WYOMING

Past and Present

Ann Byers

rosen publishing's
rosen central®

New York

Published in 2011 by The Rosen Publishing Group, Inc.
29 East 21st Street, New York, NY 10010

Library of Congress Cataloging-in-Publication Data

Wyoming: past and present / Ann Byers. — 1st ed.
        p. cm. — (The United States: past and present)
Includes bibliographical references and index.
ISBN 978-1-4358-9500-3 (library binding)
ISBN 978-1-4358-9527-0 (pbk.)
ISBN 978-1-4358-9561-4 (6-pack)
1. Wyoming—Juvenile literature. I. Title.
F761.3.B94 2011
978.7—dc22

2010002519

Manufactured in Malaysia

CPSIA Compliance Information: Batch #S10YA: For further information, contact Rosen Publishing, New York, New York, at 1-800-237-9932.

On the cover: Top left: Traders, soldiers, and Native Americans congregate at Fort Laramie. Top right: This Wyoming cow is equipped with a GPS collar to keep it within the ranch's rangeland. Bottom: These beautiful mountains are in the Teton Range in Grand Teton National Park in northwestern Wyoming.

Contents

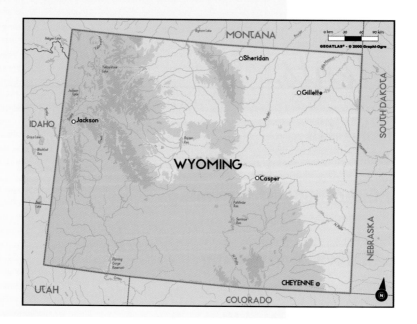

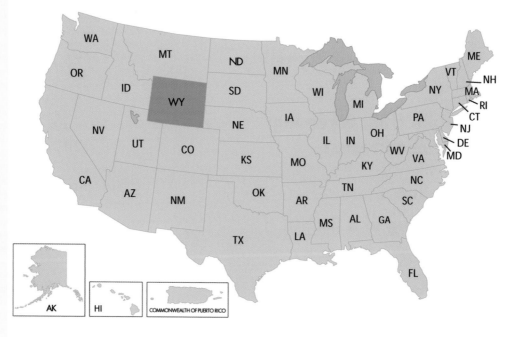

Wyoming has no natural boundaries marking its borders, so its square shape was drawn along latitude and longitude lines instead. Wyoming is the tenth largest state by area, but it's the smallest in population.

Introduction

Spectacular beauty, exciting adventure, and the enduring values of America—all are part of the great state of Wyoming. Few other U.S. states mirror the grandeur and history of the entire country so clearly. Wyoming has towering peaks and vast, windswept flatlands, ice-cold streams, and sweltering deserts. Its beauty conceals rich natural resources, including coal, gas, and oil.

The history of Wyoming is much like the story of the original thirteen colonies, complete with Native Americans, explorers, and settlers. People came to Wyoming in search of freedom, fortune, and adventure. They found all three.

The symbol of the state is a lone cowboy on a bucking horse. This image depicts the values shared by both Wyoming and America as a whole: rugged individualism, hard work, equality for all, and the unshakable belief in the right to life, liberty, and the pursuit of happiness. Wyoming is not nicknamed the Equality State and the Cowboy State for nothing!

Chapter 1

THE GEOGRAPHY OF WYOMING

Although it is the tenth largest state in terms of area, Wyoming has the smallest population. It has no natural boundaries, such as rivers, marking its borders. Instead, its nearly square shape was drawn along latitude and longitude lines. Wyoming is bordered on the north by Montana, on the east by South Dakota and Nebraska, on the south by Colorado, on the southwest corner by Utah, and on the west by Idaho.

The state has three types of physical features: mountains, basins, and plains. Some of the Rockies occupy the western two-thirds of Wyoming. In the far northeast corner of the state is a portion of the Black Hills. The Continental Divide, an imaginary line that runs through the mountains from the Arctic Ocean to the southern tip of South America, cuts across the state. The rivers to the east of the Divide flow to the Missouri Basin and then on to the Atlantic Ocean. The waters to the west of the Divide drain to the Pacific.

Among and between the mountains are basins, or shallow, bowl-like hollows of land. These are lower, relatively flat areas. They are like valleys, except they are generally wider.

The eastern third of the state is part of the Great Plains, a grassy plateau that covers much of the Midwest. The name "Wyoming" means "large plain" in the language of the Munsee Native Americans (a Delaware tribe and part of the Algonquian language group). The Wyoming Territory was named by a Congressional representative from Ohio who was familiar with its namesake—the Wyoming Valley— in neighboring Pennsylvania.

National Parks

About half of Wyoming's land has been preserved as national parks, monuments, and forests. The very first national park in the United States, Yellowstone, was established in 1872 in the northwest corner of Wyoming. Occupying more than 2 million acres (1 million hectares), the park is famous for its geysers, bison, elk, and bear. In Grand

The Snake River wends its way through Yellowstone National Park in the autumn.

Teton National Park, just south of Yellowstone, magnificent, jagged peaks tower above broad valleys and glacial lakes.

A national monument is smaller than a national park. Wyoming has two national monuments. Devils Tower is a massive, flattopped rock column that stands 1,267 feet (386 meters) above the valley of the Belle Fourche River. This, the first ever U.S. national monument, is in the Black Hills. It was featured in the 1977 movie *Close Encounters of the Third Kind*.

Wyoming's other national monument, Fossil Butte, is in the south-east corner of the state. The butte is part of an 8,198-acre (3,318-ha)

The Old Faithful geyser ejects thousands of gallons of boiling water and steam into the sky at Yellowstone National Park about every ninety minutes. The water can reach an average height of 145 feet (44 m).

park. It was once a lake brimming with life, but it eventually dried up and was pushed up by earth movements. It contains millions of fossilized plants, insects, fish, turtles, birds, and bats.

Five national forests occupy 8 million acres (3 million ha) of Wyoming. Four are named for the mountains in which they are found: Bighorn, Black Hills, Bridger-Teton, and Medicine Bow. The Shoshone National Forest, the first U.S. national forest, is east of Yellowstone. The Black Hills Forest in Wyoming is only a small part of the forest that extends into South Dakota as well. A portion of Idaho's Targhee Forest is also in Wyoming. The forests contain rugged wilderness areas.

Climate

Weather in Wyoming depends on the specific locality's latitude (distance north or south) and elevation. The state's average elevation of 6,700 feet (2,042 m) gives much of the state a cool climate. Wyoming is known for its weather extremes. It has temperatures as low as -60 degrees Fahrenheit (-51 degrees Celsius) in some places and as high as 110°F (43°C) in others. The state's average rainfall ranges from 6 inches (15 centimeters) to 60 inches (152 cm), depending on the location. Wyoming is also known for high winds, powerful thunderstorms, dangerous blizzards, and punishing hailstorms.

In the mountains, summer temperatures rarely rise above 80°F (26.6°C), and winter days are often below 0°F (-18°C). Snow can fall at any time, summer or winter. Some peaks are always covered with snow or glaciers. The basins are at least ten to fifteen degrees warmer than the mountains. Warm winds called chinooks sometimes blow down the eastern slopes. In the Bighorn Basin and the Red Desert of the Great Divide Basin, temperatures can rise above 100°F (36°C). The Plains also have hot summers, averaging 80°F to 90°F (27°C to 32°C). But temperatures drop sharply at night.

Plants

The warmer temperatures and relatively flat terrain of the Plains make eastern Wyoming a prairie—a large and treeless grassland. To the west of the Great Plains, the basins are large, dry areas with longer grasses. Sagebrush is abundant. Parts of two of the basins are desert shrublands. These arid regions have only sagebrush, greasewood, cacti, and other desert shrubs. The dry shrubs often break

Where the Buffalo Roam

Although they are of the same family as the cape buffalo of Africa and the water buffalo of Asia, American bison are not really buffalo. Historians say that as many as sixty-five million bison once occupied much of North America. Some Native Americans lived off the bison, using their hides for clothing and shelter, their meat for food, and their horns for arrowheads. They used every part of the animal, killing it only when necessary. European settlers, however, slaughtered large numbers of bison to make and sell fur robes, to feed workers building railroads, for sport, and to make room for their cattle and their homes. By 1895, only about eight hundred bison were left.

Even within the sanctuary of Yellowstone National Park and guarded by the U.S. Army, endangered bison continued to be hunted by poachers. In 1894, the U.S. Congress passed the Lacey Act, making killing bison illegal and subject to a $1,000 fine. But outside Yellowstone, the animals were still hunted for their meat and hides.

In 1886, zoologist William Hornaday, on a mission for the Smithsonian Institute, was appalled to realize how close to extinction the bison were. With then-president Theodore Roosevelt, Hornaday founded the American Bison Society in 1905. The society inspired a movement to protect the animals. The movement was opposed by commercial hunters and by people who thought that getting rid of all bison would free up the land for "progress." The movement was successful in establishing a number of wildlife refuges and state preserves where the small herds were saved and protected.

Today, in addition to the twenty thousand animals protected on public lands in the United States and Canada, nearly two hundred thousand bison are raised on private ranches. They are prized for their meat, which is leaner and healthier than beef.

from their roots and are caught by the ever-present wind, becoming tumbleweeds.

By contrast, Wyoming's mountains are thick with evergreen trees. In fact, the Black Hills were so named because the dense ponderosa pine and fir forests make the mountains look black from a distance. The western mountains are covered with lodgepole pine, Douglas fir, and Engleman spruce. Piñon pine and juniper trees also grow in the mountains. Oak trees and aspens can be found at the lower mountain elevations, and cottonwoods grow along mountain riverbanks.

Some of Wyoming's mountains are as high as 13,000 feet (3,962 m), which is above the tree line. The climate above 9,500 feet (2,896 m) is called alpine tundra. Only grasses and herbs poke through the snow at this elevation.

Animals

The short grasses of Wyoming's plains nourish animals that graze: bison, cattle, and sheep. The leafy shrubs of the basins and the woody plants of the lower mountain elevations are perfect for animals that browse: deer, goats, and pronghorn antelope. More than four hundred thousand pronghorn—half the world's population—live in Wyoming. These areas are also the habitat of foxes, bobcats, coyotes, jackrabbits, cottontails, prairie dogs, ferrets, and other small animals.

The mountains are home to larger creatures. Elk and bighorn sheep climb high during the summer and come down to lower elevations in the winter. Grizzly and black bears roam the western mountains, and moose live in the northwestern ranges. Deer, especially mule deer, are in the mountains as well as the lowlands. Wolves,

Bison forage for winter food in Yellowstone National Park. They are the largest mammals in the park but are vegetarians, eating only grasses and sedges.

at one time very common, became nearly extinct as ranchers hunted them to protect their livestock. In 1995, they were reintroduced into Yellowstone, and their numbers are growing.

In the mountains, large predatory birds soar: hawks, falcons, ravens, and eagles. On the Plains, game birds scurry about: sage hens, grouse, wild turkeys, and quail. In the rivers and streams, waterfowl glide: ducks, geese, swans, white pelicans, and cranes. The cold streams and lakes of the high mountains contain six kinds of trout. The warmer lakes and waterways of the basins support a variety of other game fish. Wyoming may have relatively few people, but its wildlife is plentiful!

Chapter 2

THE HISTORY OF WYOMING

The story of Wyoming is a tale of rugged people attempting to tame a rugged land. Hardy explorers and adventurers came west looking for the "Western Sea," the gold of California, and free land being offered in Oregon. On their way, they discovered a wild but beautiful territory. A number of them chose to settle there.

Early Exploration

The first Europeans to explore the northern Rockies were French Canadian fur trappers who paddled down the area's rivers looking for beavers. The Verendrye brothers discovered the Bighorn Mountains in 1742. In 1807, the American John Colter reached western Wyoming and amazed easterners with his hard-to-believe descriptions of the geysers of Yellowstone.

For the next half century, Wyoming remained an unsettled wilderness. A few forts were scattered along trade routes, but they were little more than way stations where fur trappers could rest and stock up on supplies. By 1840, most of the beavers were gone along with demand for their pelts. No one had any reason to make the arduous journey to Wyoming any longer.

A wagon train travels on the Oregon Trail at Devil's Gate, Wyoming, on its way to the free land of the Oregon Territory in this painting by W. H. Jackson.

Passing Through

The fur trade had sparked interest in lands farther west of what would become Wyoming, however. Trappers had seen the Oregon Territory—present-day Washington, Oregon, Idaho, and parts of western Montana and Wyoming. The South Pass through the Rockies in Wyoming made overland travel from the eastern states to this Northwest Territory possible. In 1832, Captain Benjamin Bonneville took twenty wagons filled with 110 men over South Pass to the Oregon Territory. Ten years later, Elijah White led the first party of settlers over the same route, which became known as the Oregon Trail.

A number of events made the migration westward very popular. Economic woes in the east and a spirit of adventure drove many families to seek their fortunes in the Oregon Territory. Religious persecution pushed Mormon families out of Illinois and through Wyoming. Discoveries of gold—first in California and then in Colorado, Montana, and the Black Hills—brought others. The 1850 offer of free land to settlers in the Oregon Territory clinched the deal for many. Few of these settlers and fortune hunters, however, were staying in Wyoming. They were just passing through.

Sitting Bull was a Hunkpapa Lakota Sioux who was considered a holy man by his people. He accurately predicted his forces' victory over General Custer at Little Bighorn.

Conflicts with Native Americans

Though the people heading west were merely passing through Wyoming, the land they traveled across was inhabited by long-term, full-time residents. A number of Native American tribes lived as nomads there, following the bison. They had been friendly with the fur trappers who came a few at a time. Once wagon trains of hundreds of people arrived, however, their welcoming attitude changed. The wagons trampled the grasses that the bison depended on for food, the people threw their trash in the clear streams, and they killed hundreds of animals.

Cheyenne

The capital of Wyoming, like many of the other major cities of the state, began as a railroad town. When officials of the Union Pacific chose this location, they called it Cheyenne after one of the Native American groups in the area. To protect the crews constructing the tracks against attacks from Indians, the U.S. Army built Fort Russell nearby. From July to November 1867, about four thousand men lived in tents and either laid track or furnished supplies to those who did. When the tracks were finished two years later, some people stayed.

Cheyenne was a typical Wild West town. Saloons and burlesque theaters were everywhere. But the railroad soon turned the rough and scrappy community into a major business hub. It also brought families from the East to settle the frontier, and with them came stability, culture, and the latest styles. Cheyenne became like a refined eastern city set in the mountains of the West.

Once the army succeeded in clearing the Plains of bison and Indians, fortunes could be made raising cattle. Wealthy people from the eastern states and from Europe came to Wyoming for this purpose. They became known as "cattle barons." They built the posh Cheyenne Club, modeled after English country clubs, where the "royalty" of the West gathered for card games, billiards, conversation, and expensive food.

From the very beginning, Cheyenne was the largest and most modern town in Wyoming. Today, it remains the state's biggest city and its capital. Instead of cattle ranchers, the major employer there is now the U.S. government. After World War II (1941–1945), Fort Russell, once the largest cavalry outpost in the country, became the Francis E. Warren Air Force Base. It was the first base in the United States to house nuclear missiles. Since 1958, many of the nation's intercontinental ballistic missiles (ICBMs) have been located at Warren.

To keep the tensions on both sides from erupting into war, representatives of the United States and several Indian nations signed the Treaty of Fort Laramie in 1851. The United States promised to pay the tribes $50,000 per year, and the tribes agreed to allow the United States to build roads and forts along the Oregon Trail and let the wagon trains pass in safety.

Neither side honored the treaty, and battles followed. When Chief Red Cloud objected to the presence of some U.S. Army forts, the Indians attacked and defeated the American forces. In the Second Treaty of Fort Laramie (1868), the United States agreed to allow the tribes to govern themselves without interference on the Great Sioux Reservation. The federal government also acknowledged the Indians' right to hunting grounds throughout Wyoming.

In 1874, however, gold was discovered in the Black Hills. These hills were part of the Great Sioux Reservation. Ignoring the terms of the 1868 treaty, prospectors poured into the area, and the U.S. Army tried to protect them. Chiefs Sitting Bull and Crazy Horse resisted the violation of their territory, defeating General George Custer at the Battle of Little Bighorn. Eventually, the larger and better armed forces of the United States prevailed, and all the tribes were forced onto reservations.

Settlement

With the threat of Indian attacks removed, settlers slowly ventured into the Wyoming Territory. First came the railroad workers, racing to lay track for a rail line that would span the continent. Workers of the Union Pacific built the stretch across Wyoming from July 1867 to mid-1869. Wherever they worked, small towns cropped up. Some of

As part of its westward expansion, the Union Pacific Railroad laid tracks through southern Wyoming in 1867 and 1868. In this photograph, the temporary "end of the line" reaches Archer, Wyoming, a town named for an engineer who helped survey for the railroad.

the towns along the construction route grew into permanent settlements.

Cattle ranchers soon discovered the good rangelands in Wyoming. The transcontinental railroad made it easy for the ranchers to ship meat to markets in the East. This resulted in many cattlemen moving in and settling Wyoming's rangelands.

After the Homestead Act offered buyers cheap land throughout the West, more settlers began trickling into Wyoming. Many of these homesteaders were small-scale ranchers, raising just a few hundred head of cattle. Violent conflicts frequently arose between the large-operation cattlemen and the smaller ones. The largest of the range wars, the Johnson County Cattle War, ended only after President Benjamin Harrison sent in the cavalry.

Peace gradually came to the Wild West and with it more people. But Wyoming never had a settlement boom like that of the Oregon Territory. When the first census was taken in 1870, the population of the entire state was only 9,118.

Statehood

At various times, four different countries laid claim to all or parts of what finally became the state of Wyoming. The United States bought the portion east of the Continental Divide from France as part of the Louisiana Purchase. The northwest corner was part of land that England agreed to give the United States, and the southwest corner was ceded by Mexico. A small section in the south was obtained from the Republic of Texas, which was then a breakaway area of Mexico that eventually became the U.S. state of Texas. By 1850, all of the land that would form the state of Wyoming belonged to the United States.

At that time, much of the western United States was organized into territories. In 1868, the Wyoming Territory was created from the Dakota, Utah, and Idaho territories. A territory had a government and a constitution, but it could not become a state until it had sixty thousand inhabitants. In 1868, the Wyoming Territory had barely nine thousand. Twenty-two years later, on July 10, 1890, Wyoming, with a population of 62,553, became the forty-fourth state of the Union.

Chapter 3

THE GOVERNMENT OF WYOMING

When Wyoming became a state, its population was so small that it was organized into only five counties. Today, it has twenty-three. It is still so sparsely populated, however, that it only has one representative in the U.S. House of Representatives. Thus, the tenth largest state by area has only three votes (one for each representative and each of the two senators) in the electoral college that selects the president of the United States.

The government of Wyoming is very similar to the federal government. It consists of three branches. These branches of the state government are the legislative (which makes laws), the executive (which carries out the laws), and the judicial (which makes sure the laws are constitutional and carried out fairly).

Legislative Branch

As in the federal government, Wyoming's legislature has two houses. The house of representatives has sixty members that are elected for two-year terms. The senate has thirty members who serve four-year terms.

Unlike the federal government, Wyoming has a citizen legislature, rather than a professional legislature. That means the state senators and representatives work only part-time in state government. They meet as a group only once a year. In odd-numbered years, they meet in general session for no more than forty days. In even-numbered years, they meet for a budget session for about twenty days. Between the yearly meetings, the governor may call special sessions.

Legislators also work in committees. Each house has the same twelve standing committees that study issues and write laws to present at the next general session. House and senate members can form joint interim committees. They are "joint" because members of both houses meet together, and "interim" because they meet between regular sessions.

The rotunda of the state capitol in Cheyenne is made of stained glass imported from England. The rotunda is ringed by the offices of four of the five executive officers of Wyoming.

Executive Branch

When a bill proposed by the state legislature becomes law, the governor has the responsibility of enforcing it. He or she is the chief executive officer. Wyoming has five executive officers, each elected for a four-year term. These are the governor, secretary of state, auditor, treasurer, and superintendent of public instruction. The governor makes sure all the departments of the state are functioning properly and appoints leaders of the forty state agencies. The governor

Wyoming Women and Politics

Nicknamed the Equality State, Wyoming was the first U.S. state to treat women as the equals of men. It was the first place in the nation where a woman could vote and where women served on a jury. The first female judge in the nation, the first woman to be elected to state office, and the first female governor were all from Wyoming. However, those achievements did not come easily.

Long before Wyoming became a state, in 1869, the territorial legislature passed a law granting women the right to vote. Some legislators hoped to attract females to the state, where men outnumbered women eight to one. But not everyone was happy with the decision. Two years later, some legislators tried to repeal the law. They lost by one vote. When Wyoming applied for admission to the Union, the senator from Alabama objected because he didn't want Wyoming's notion of equality for women to "pollute" the thinking of the rest of the country.

Today, Wyoming women have risen to positions of leadership at the national and state level. In 2008—140 years after Wyoming first extended equal rights to women—23 percent of the state's legislators were women. One of the state's two representatives to the House of Representatives in Washington, D.C., the state auditor, and one state supreme court judge were all women. Since Wyoming became a state, women have served in all five elected state executive positions and in several circuit courts.

Women line up to cast their ballots in Cheyenne in 1888, thirty-two years before American women "got the vote" nationwide.

presents the state's budget to the legislature and serves as commander in chief of the Wyoming Army and Air National Guard.

When the governor is out of the state, the secretary of state is the acting governor. This is the person who keeps the official state records. The secretary of state keeps the public informed about what is happening in the state.

Wyoming has two financial officers: a treasurer and an auditor. The treasurer is like a banker, taking in money and investing it. The auditor oversees how the state spends its money. Unlike many states, Wyoming has no individual income tax and no taxes on businesses. Funds necessary to run the government come from three sources: sales tax; property taxes; and taxes on mineral extraction, or mining.

The fifth elected executive is the superintendent of public instruction. This person is responsible for the performance of all the public schools (from kindergarten through twelfth grade) and the rules governing them.

Judicial Branch

Wyoming judges are first appointed, serve their term, and then face a public election to return them to their post. For each position, a nominating committee gives the governor a list of three lawyers. The governor chooses one from this list. When a judge's term is up, the people vote whether to keep that judge in office or not. Judges may remain in office until age seventy, as long as the people vote to retain them.

The lowest level of court is the circuit court. Circuit court judges serve four-year terms and preside over minor matters—lawsuits that

The state supreme court building in Cheyenne was recently renovated. During the work, court sessions were held in the former offices of the department of health.

involve less than $7,000, misdemeanor crimes, and family violence cases. In some remote areas, part-time magistrates who are not law-yers may substitute for judges if necessary.

Larger cases—felonies and bigger lawsuits—are handled in district courts. People who are not happy with a decision of the circuit court can appeal to the district court. Wyoming is divided into nine districts, and twenty-one judges serve those districts. Their terms last six years.

Wyoming's highest court is the state supreme court. The five supreme court justices hear appeals from the lower courts. They serve eight-year terms. One of them acts as chief justice for a four-year term.

Chapter 4

THE ECONOMY OF
WYOMING

Much like the bucking horse that is the state's symbol, the economy of Wyoming has had several wild ups and downs. The first big economic boom was the fur trade of the early 1800s. By 1840, however, demand for fur had dropped, and the trapping economy collapsed. Cattle brought the second major boom. But the blizzard of 1887–1888, a large influx of settlers, and the overgrazing of rangeland brought that industry down. Through much of the 1900s, the state's major export product was oil. But when oil prices fell in 1982, the economy suffered greatly. Today, the economy of Wyoming has three main sectors: mining, agriculture, and tourism.

Mining

The largest sector of the state's economy is mining. Wyoming leads the nation in coal production, is second in natural gas, and is sixth in output of oil, or petroleum. The state also has the world's largest deposit of trona, which is processed into bicarbonate of soda. Bicarbonate is used as baking soda and in making chemicals, glass, paper, and soap. The trona mined in southwest Wyoming supplies 90 percent of the nation's needs. Other Wyoming mining products are uranium, gold, iron, and clay.

Agriculture

The agricultural sector includes crops and livestock, or animals. Most of the land in Wyoming is devoted to raising livestock. The state has 1.4 million cattle and calves—almost three times its human population! More money is made on cattle than any other farm product. The best grazing land, including acreage in some national parks, is reserved for cattle. Lower-quality pasture is used for raising sheep. Wyoming also produces hogs, dairy products, wool, eggs, and honey.

Here, coal is being extracted from a strip mine. Wyoming is the country's leading producer of coal.

Only 4 percent of the land area of the state is used for growing crops. Most of that is in the Plains of the east and in the Bighorn and Wind River basins. The largest crop, by volume, is hay used to feed livestock. Other major crops are sugar beets, wheat, barley, beans, and corn for livestock. Oats and sunflowers are also grown.

Tourism

Wyoming seems custom-made for tourism. Five national parks and recreation areas and ten national forests cover 11 million acres (4 million ha). Every year, millions of people from all over the world

Cattle Ranching

Cattle are not native to Wyoming. But after the area's bison herds were destroyed, some cattlemen recognized that the vast, empty plain of eastern Wyoming was good grazing country. Cows were soon brought from Texas, and from the mid-1800s until about 1930, the cattle roamed the open range. At first, cowboys simply branded them, let them graze freely, and collected them at roundup time. They then drove them to the railheads for shipment to the markets in the East.

Today, cattle no longer roam the open range. Although there are still some large properties, the average cattle ranch consists of less than 3,000 acres (1,214 ha). The smaller operations are much more efficient. The cattle do not die when harsh winters kill the prairie grasses because mechanization has allowed ranchers to store hay for these times. Today's cows receive minerals and other nutritional supplements, and most are fed corn at least part of the year. This fattens them up two to three times faster than grasses. The industry is no longer a matter of survival of the fittest. Breeding programs help ranchers develop strong stock, and vaccinations keep the animals free of disease. Many of the ranches specialize, raising cattle for purebred Angus beef, all-natural beef, or other niche markets.

Electronic technology is also changing life on the range. Some ranchers are fitting their cows with global positioning system (GPS) devices. These boxlike units are placed on the animal's head and programmed with the coordinates that mark the limits of the ranch. If a cow ventures close to those limits, the GPS device emits sounds that coax the cow to stay within the unseen electronic fence. Today's cowboys, with their pickup trucks and cell phones, no longer need lassos to nudge their little dogies to "git" along!

Haney Stephenson has 3,500 head of Angus cattle on his ranch near Alcova.

Visitors ride in a horse-drawn sleigh to see elk at the National Elk Refuge in Jackson.

come to Wyoming to enjoy its beauty. Rodeos, Wild West shows, cattle roundups, and frontier celebrations draw visitors from across the country and the entire globe. The dude ranches scattered throughout the state also attract travelers bent on a more adventurous vacation. In all, tourists contribute more than $1 billion to the state's economy every year.

Outlook

Since the turn of the century, the economic statistics for Wyoming have been better than those for the nation as a whole. Job growth has been greater, unemployment lower, and income higher. The state has three economic strengths: no taxes for businesses, low energy costs, and an abundance of natural energy resources. On the other hand, Wyoming has two disadvantages. First, most of the jobs are in only a few industries. Second, the majority of money earned comes from jobs in the energy field, where prices drastically fluctuate. If the price of oil and natural gas goes up, Wyoming residents do well. If it drops, their incomes fall. Wyoming's economic history will likely continue, like the bucking bronco, to be a wild ride.

Chapter 5

PEOPLE FROM WYOMING:
PAST AND PRESENT

Wyoming has produced many famous and accomplished warriors and military men, athletes, entertainers, authors, lawyers, and politicians. These are just a few of the proud sons and daughters of the Equality State.

Richard (Dick) Cheney (1941–) After earning bachelor's and master's degrees from the University of Wyoming, Dick Cheney went into politics. He served in various roles under presidents Richard Nixon and Gerald Ford. When Ford lost his bid for a second term, Cheney returned to Wyoming and was elected to his state's only seat in the House of Representatives. He served six terms. Under President George H. W. Bush, Cheney served as secretary of defense (1989–1993). From 2001 to 2009, he was vice president of the United States under the former President Bush's son, George W. Bush.

"Buffalo" Bill Cody (1846–1914) Having become fatherless at age eleven, Bill Cody worked as a messenger boy with a wagon train, a mail carrier for the Pony Express, and an army scout. He hunted buffalo to supply meat to railroad

William Frederick Cody earned his nickname Buffalo Bill by hunting and killing large numbers of buffalo to help feed railroad workers laying track through Wyoming. Cody was also an army scout and carnival showman.

construction crews, and he guided people on buffalo hunting expeditions. After appearing in a play loosely based on his adventures, Cody put together "Buffalo Bill's Wild West," a traveling circus-like show. The show toured the country as well as parts of Europe. The Iowa native founded the town of Cody, Wyoming.

Matthew Fox (1966–)
Born in Pennsylvania, Matthew Fox was raised on the Bitterroot Ranch outside Dubois, in Wyoming. With a degree in economics, he set out to become a Wall Street

Though born in Pennsylvania, actor Matthew Fox grew up on a longhorn cattle ranch near Dubois.

stock trader. A brief stint at modeling led to TV commercials, and Fox became hooked on acting. His big break came at age twenty-five, when he landed a part in an episode of the TV show *Wings*. After playing a number of small roles, he gained recognition as Charlie Salinger in *Party of Five*. Today, he is best known as Dr. Jack Shephard in the popular TV series *Lost*.

Rulon Gardner (1971–) Hard work on a family dairy farm in Afton, Wyoming, and sparring with eight older

J. C. Penney

The seventh of twelve children in a Missouri farming family, James Cash Penney (1875–1971) learned the value of hard work early in life. At the age of eight, he earned money to pay for his school clothes. He also learned to live by the Golden Rule: "Do unto others as you would have them do unto you."

At twenty-seven, Penney was working in a Colorado dry goods store called, appropriately enough, the Golden Rule. The owner offered to make him a partner. With $500 in savings, Penney took out a loan and moved to Kemmerer, Wyoming, to start his very own Golden Rule.

At that time, Kemmerer was a coal mining town of a thousand people with one store and twenty-one saloons. The store was a company store—owned by the mine operators. They sold their goods on credit and charged very high interest. Penney refused to operate with credit. His store accepted cash only in an attempt to protect his customers from crushing debt and huge interest payments. He determined that his store would be true to its name: J. C. Penney would treat his customers as he would wish to be treated. He would sell quality merchandise at fair prices.

The first day's receipts totaled $466.89 (mostly in coins), nearly enough to repay the amount of money Penney had invested from his own savings. Within ten years, Penney had thirty-four Golden Rule stores. By 1929, he had 1,400 across the country. He bought out his partners and changed the stores' name to the J. C. Penney Company.

With the success, Penney also had heartaches. Two wives died very young. His business faltered in the stock market crash of 1929. But he always rebounded. The company has since had a number of ups and downs, but it, too, has always rebounded. Today, J. C. Penney is the largest department store retailer in the United States. It has the largest apparel and home furnishing sites on the Internet and the nation's largest general merchandise catalog business. There are 1,109 stores in operation, with annual revenues approaching $20 billion. The "mother store" in Kemmerer is still in operation.

siblings made Rulon Gardner strong. A Greco-Roman wrestler, he won Olympic bronze and gold medals, beating an opponent previously undefeated for thirteen years. Gardner overcame a learning disability to earn a college degree in physical education. He survived an arrow wound and snowmobile, motorcycle, and airplane accidents. Now retired from wrestling, Gardner is a motivational speaker, using his experiences to inspire others to persevere and realize their dreams.

Curt Gowdy (1919–2006) As a broadcaster in New York, Curt Gowdy (born in Green River) was called the Cowboy at the Mike. His announcing career began with a radio broadcast of a six-man football game in Cheyenne. Over the next sixty years, he delivered the play-by-play for sixteen World Series, twelve Rose Bowls, nine Super Bowls, sixteen All-Star Games, eight Olympic Games, and twenty-four NCAA Final Fours. He also hosted *The American Sportsman* television program. Gowdy was inducted into twenty different sports, broadcasting, conservation, and fishing halls of fame.

Patricia MacLachlan (1938–) As a child in Cheyenne and later in Minnesota, Patricia MacLachlan always had her nose in a book. She read stories, acted them out, and made up tales of her own. She became a junior high English teacher and a social worker for foster mothers. When she began writing at age thirty-five, she penned picture books for young children. Then she ventured into stories for older children. Of her many award-winning books, the most well known are

Nellie Tayloe Ross was elected governor of Wyoming in 1925, following the death of the sitting governor, her husband, William Ross. She was the first woman in the United States to be elected governor of a state. She lived to the age of 101 and is buried in Cheyenne.

Sarah, Plain and Tall and its sequels, all set in the plains of Wyoming.

Nellie Tayloe Ross (1876–1977) Nellie Ross was a school-teacher, not a politician. But when her husband, William Ross, the governor of Wyoming, died in office, the Democratic Party nominated her to fill his position. Although she did not campaign, she won and became the first woman governor of any state. She was not reelected but remained active in politics. President Franklin Roosevelt appointed her head of the U.S. Mint—another first for a woman—and she held the position for twenty years.

Gerald (Gerry) Spence (1929–) Wyoming born and bred, Gerald Spence (born in Laramie) achieved national fame as a trial lawyer. He won a judgment against a chemical company in the death of Karen Silkwood. The events surrounding this case were later depicted in an Oscar-nominated movie starring Meryl Streep. Spence also won a case brought against the federal government over an incident at Ruby Ridge, Idaho, involving a deadly siege of a suspected white suprem-acist's home and property by the FBI and U.S. Marshals. In 1990, Spence defended Imelda Marcos, widow of the deposed president of the Philippines, Ferdinand Marcos. She was facing racketeering and fraud charges related to her and her husband's apparently illegal amassing of enormous personal wealth at the public's expense. He has never lost a criminal case, either as a prosecutor or a defense lawyer. Spence founded the Trial Lawyers College in Dubois, Wyoming, to train others to fight for justice for "the poor, the forgotten, and the defenseless."

Washakie (c. 1808–1900) The name "Washakie," or "Rattle," came from a device the Shoshone warrior carried with him into battle to frighten the horses of his enemies. More than a fierce warrior, Chief Washakie was a friend of the white trappers and soldiers in the Wyoming Territory. He allied himself and his braves with the white settlers against the larger Sioux and

A leader of the Eastern Shoshone, Chief Washakie was renowned for both his skill in battle and his efforts to make peace. He is the only Native American for whom a U.S. military outpost was named, Fort Washakie.

Cheyenne tribes. He gave his daughter in marriage to the fur trader James Bridger, served as a scout for the U.S. Army, and fought alongside U.S. General George Crook in the Battle of the Rosebud. He is the only Indian chief to be buried with full U.S. military honors.

Owen Wister (1860–1938) He was not from Wyoming and was not a cattleman, but Owen Wister popularized the cowboy. Born into a wealthy Philadelphia family, Wister graduated from Harvard and became a lawyer. Of the many places he traveled—including France, Britain, and Switzerland—he loved Wyoming best. His 1902 novel, *The Virginian*, gave the rest of the country a romanticized picture of life in the Wild West and made the Wyoming cowboy an American hero. The book has been reprinted numerous times and has been made into a stage production, four movies, and a television series.

Timeline

1742–1743	The Verendrye brothers are probably the first Europeans to enter Wyoming.
1803	Through the Louisiana Purchase, the United States buys land from France that includes part of present-day Wyoming.
1832	Captain Benjamin Bonneville takes 110 men and 20 wagons through South Pass.
1846	The Oregon Territory, including northwest Wyoming, is ceded to the United States by the British.
1848	The United States acquires southwest Wyoming through Mexican cessation.
1850	The United States obtains the final portion of present-day Wyoming from the Republic of Texas.
1862	The Homestead Act offers land in western territories to settlers.
1867–1869	Track for the Union Pacific Railroad is laid through Wyoming.
1868	Congress creates the Territory of Wyoming on July 25.
1869	Wyoming's territorial government grants women the right to vote.
1870	Women serve on juries in Laramie, the first to do so in the United States.
1872	Yellowstone Wonderland is established as the world's first national park.
1876	General George Custer is killed in the Battle of Little Bighorn.
1884	Wyoming's first oil well is drilled.
1890	Wyoming is admitted to the Union as the forty-fourth state on July 10.
1892	The Johnson County Cattle War rages in Wyoming.
1906	Devils Tower National Monument is established.
1918	Uranium is discovered in Wyoming.
1924	Nellie Ross becomes governor of Wyoming, the first elected female governor in the United States.
2001	Dick Cheney is sworn in as vice president of the United States.
2010	Development of wind energy is precluded (forbidden) on more than 20 percent of Wyoming land to protect the habitat of the threatened sage grouse.

State motto:	"Equal Rights"
State capital:	Cheyenne
State tree:	Plains cottonwood
State flower:	Wyoming Indian Paintbrush
State bird:	Western meadowlark
State dinosaur:	Triceratops
State gem:	Jade
Statehood date and number:	July 10, 1890; forty-fourth state
State nicknames:	Officially, the Equality State; popularly, the Cowboy State
Total area and U.S. rank:	97,814 square miles (253,337 sq km); tenth-largest state
Population:	522,830
Highest elevation:	Gannett Peak in the Wind River Mountain Range, at 13,804 feet (4,207 m)
Lowest elevation:	Belle Fourche River Valley in the state's northeast corner, at 3,125 feet (953 m)

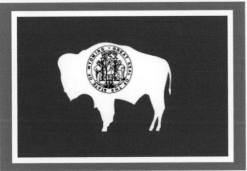

State flag

State seal

Major rivers:	North Platte River, Big Horn River, Wind River, Yellowstone River, Snake River, Green River
Major lakes:	Yellowstone Lake, Glendo Reservoir, Bighorn Lake, Boysen Reservoir, Flaming Gorge Reservoir, Seminoe Reservoir, Alcova Reservoir, Keyhole Reservoir
Hottest recorded temperature:	114°F (46°C), at Basin (in Big Horn Basin), July 12, 1900
Coldest recorded temperature:	-66°F (-54°C), at Yellowstone, February 9, 1933
Origin of state name:	Munsee (Delaware) Indian word meaning "great plains;" the Wyoming Territory was named after the Wyoming Valley in Pennsylvania
Chief agricultural products:	Beef, alfalfa hay, sugar beets, barley, corn, wheat, oats, beans
Major industries:	Oil and gas extraction, coal and trona mining, cattle and sheep raising, tourism

Western meadowlark

Wyoming Indian paintbrush

GLOSSARY

browse To eat mostly leaves.

butte A hill that stands by itself, usually with steep sides and a flattened top.

chinook A warm, dry wind that blows down the eastern slopes of the Rocky Mountains.

extraction The act of taking one material out of another. Mineral extraction is the process of mining, or taking minerals out of the ground.

graze To eat mostly grasses.

interim The period of time between two events.

latitude The distance on Earth's surface north or south of the equator.

longitude The distance east or west on Earth's surface, measured by lines that extend from the North to the South Pole.

magistrate A local official given authority to perform administrative and sometimes judicial functions, though often not technically qualified for such tasks.

mineral Nonliving material that occurs naturally in the ground, such as coal.

plateau A large stretch of elevated and relatively flat land.

prairie A large area of level or slightly rolling grassland with few, if any, trees.

railhead Point on a railroad line where supplies are loaded on or off.

reservation Land set aside, or reserved, for Native American tribes.

standing committee A more or less permanent committee, often within a legislature.

terrain An area of ground.

tree line The imaginary altitude line at about 9,500 feet (2,896 m) above which trees generally do not grow.

way station A small outpost between larger stations or cities.

Bighorn National Forest

2013 Eastside 2nd Street

Sheridan, WY 82801

(307) 674-2600

Web site: http://www.fs.fed.us/r2/bighorn

No region in Wyoming has a more diverse landscape—from lush grasslands to alpine meadows, from crystal-clear lakes to glacial carved valleys, from rolling hills to sheer mountain walls—than the Bighorn National Forest.

Bridger-Teton National Forest

P.O. Box 1888

Jackson, WY 83001

(307) 739-5500

Web site: http://www.fs.fed.us/r4/btnf

Bridger-Teton National Forest offers more than 3.4 million acres (1.3 million ha) of public land for outdoor recreation. With its pristine watersheds, abundant wildlife, and immense wildlands, it comprises a large part of the Greater Yellowstone Ecosystem—the largest intact ecosystem in the lower forty-eight states.

Devils Tower National Monument

P.O. Box 10

Devils Tower, WY 82714

(307) 467-5283

Web site: http://www.nps.gov/deto/index.htm

Devils Tower rises 1,267 feet (386 m) above the Belle Fourche River and is covered with pine forests, woodlands, and grasslands. Also known as Bears Lodge, it is a sacred site for many American Indians. President Theodore Roosevelt proclaimed Devils Tower the first national monument in 1906.

Fossil Butte National Monument

P.O. Box 592

Kemmerer, WY 83101

(307) 877-4455

Web site: http://www.nps.gov/fobu/index.htm

Some of the world's best-preserved fossils are in the flattopped ridges of southwestern Wyoming's cold sagebrush desert. Fossilized fish, insects, plants, reptiles, birds, and mammals are exceptional for their abundance, variety, and detail of preservation.

Grand Teton National Park

P.O. Drawer 170

Moose, WY 83012

(307) 739-3300

Web site: http://www.nps.gov/grte/index.htm

Grand Teton National Park preserves a spectacular landscape with majestic mountains, pristine lakes, and extraordinary wildlife. The abrupt vertical rise of the jagged Teton Range contrasts with the horizontal sage-covered valley and glacial lakes at the base, creating scenery that attracts nearly four million visitors a year.

Medicine Bow—Routt National Forests

2468 Jackson Street

Laramie, WY 82070

(307) 745-2300

Web site: http://www.fs.fed.us/r2/mbr

The Medicine Bow—Routt National Forests encompass portions of many mountain ranges, including the Gore Range, Flat Tops, Parks Range, Medicine Bow Mountains, Sierra Madre, and Laramie Range. The forests provide wildlife habitat, timber, forage for livestock, and are a vital source of water for irrigation, domestic use, and industry.

Shoshone National Forest

808 Meadowlane Avenue

Cody, WY 82414

(307) 527-6241

Web site: http://www.fs.fed.us/r2/shoshone

Set aside in 1891 as part of the Yellowstone Timberland Reserve, the Shoshone is the first national forest in the United States. It consists of some 2.4 million acres (1 million ha) of terrain ranging from sagebrush flats to rugged mountains. The forest encompasses the area from the Montana state line south to Lander, Wyoming.

University of Wyoming

1000 East University Avenue

Laramie, WY 82071

(307) 766-1121

Web site: http://www.uwyo.edu

The University of Wyoming is the state's only provider of baccalaureate and graduate education, research, and outreach services. It has more than 180 programs of study, an outstanding faculty, and world-class research facilities, all set against the idyllic backdrop of southeastern Wyoming's rugged mountains and high plains.

Wyoming Travel & Tourism

1520 Etchepare Circle

Cheyenne, WY 82007

(307) 777-7777

Web site: http://www.wyomingtourism.org

This is Wyoming's official state travel office and Web site.

Yellowstone National Park

P.O. Box 168

Yellowstone National Park, WY 82190-0168

(307) 344-7381

Web site: http://www.nps.gov/yell/index.htm

Established in 1872, Yellowstone National Park is America's first national park. Located in Wyoming, Montana, and Idaho, it is home to a large variety of wildlife, including grizzly bears, wolves, bison, and elk. Preserved within Yellowstone National Park are Old Faithful and a collection of the world's most extraordinary geysers and hot springs.

Web Sites

Due to the changing nature of Internet links, Rosen Publishing has developed an online list of Web sites related to the subject of this book. This site is updated regularly. Please use this link to access the list:

http://www.rosenlinks.com/uspp/wypp

Altsheler, Joseph A. *The Scouts of the Valley: A Story of Wyoming and the Chemung*. Gloustershire, England: Dodo Press, 2006.

Bograd, Larry. *Uniquely Wyoming*. Chicago, IL: Heinemann-Raintree, 2005.

D'Arge, Mackil. *Lifting the Sky*. New York, NY: Bloomsbury, 2009.

Hanson-Harding, Alexandra. *Wyoming* (From Sea to Shining Sea). New York, NY: Children's Press, 2008.

Marsh, Carol. *Wyoming's Native Americans: A Kid's Look at Our State's Chiefs, Tribes, Reservations, Powwows, Lore, and More from the Past to the Present*. Peachtree City, GA: Gallopade International, 2004.

Olhoff, Jim. *Wyoming* (The United States). Edina, MN: Checkerboard Books, 2009.

Prentzas, G. S. *Wyoming* (America the Beautiful). New York, NY: Scholastic, 2009.

Ryan, Pam Munoz. *Paint the Wind*. New York, NY: Scholastic, 2007.

Smith, Douglas M., and Gary Ferguson. *Decade of the Wolf: Returning the Wild to Yellowstone*. Guilford, CT: Lyons Press, 2005.

Stockton, Shreve. *The Daily Coyote: A Story of Love, Survival, and Trust in the Wilds of Wyoming*. New York, NY: Simon & Schuster, 2008.

Thomas, William David. *Wyoming* (Portraits of the States). Strongsville, OH: Gareth Stevens Publishing, 2007.

Zollman, Pam. *Wyoming* (Rookie Read-About Geography). New York, NY: Children's Press, 2007.

American Museum of Natural History. "Bison." Retrieved September 2009 (http://www.amnh.org/exhibitions/virtual/bison/history.php).

Biography.jrank.org. "Patricia MacLachlan." Retrieved October 2009 (http://biography.jrank.org/pages/2148/MacLachlan-Patricia-1938.html).

Burt, Nathaniel. *Wyoming*. Oakland, CA: Compass American Guides, 1991.

Center for American Women and Politics, Eagleton Institute of Politics. "State Fact Sheet: Wyoming." Rutgers.edu, 2009. Retrieved October 2009 (http://www.cawp.rutgers.edu/fast_facts/resources/state_fact_sheets/WY.php).

City of Kemmerer. "J. C. Penney Store/Home." Retrieved October 2009 (http://www.kemmerer.org/jcpenney.php).

Johnson, Pete. "Curt Gowdy." WomenAnglers.us, 2006. Retrieved September 2009 (http://www.womenanglers.us/Curt_Gowdy.html).

Kaeding, Beth. "History of Bison in Yellowstone National Park." National Park Service, 1997. Retrieved September 2009 (http://www.geocities.com/dmonteit/bison_hist.html).

Meagher, Margaret Mary. *The Bison of Yellowstone National Park*. Washington, DC: National Park Service Scientific Monograph Series 1, 1973.

National Bison Association. "Industry Data and Statistics." BisonCentral.com, 2009. Retrieved September 2009 (http://www.bisoncentral.com/bison-reources-information.php?c=14&d=105&a=1064&w=2&r=Y).

Pitcher, Don. *Wyoming* (Moon Handbooks). 6th ed. Emeryville, CA: Avalon, 2006.

Reese, Alice Anna, and Carlynn Trout. "Famous Missourians: James Cash Penney." State Historical Society of Missouri. Retrieved October 2009 (http://shs.umsystem.edu/famousmissourians/entrepreneurs/penney/penney.shtml).

SharpShooter. "What It's Like to Manage a Modern Ranch." Hubpages.com. Retrieved September 2009 (http://hubpages.com/hub/modern-ranching).

About the Author

Ann Byers is a youth worker, editor, and writer. She and her husband live in California. From there, they enjoy traveling throughout the western states, including Wyoming.

Photo Credits

Cover (top left), p. 14 MPI/Hulton Archive/Getty Images; cover (top right) Dave Ganskopp/USDA; cover (bottom) pp. 3, 6, 13, 20, 25, 29, 38 Shutterstock.com; p. 4 © GeoAtlas; p. 7 © www.istockphoto.com/James Brey; p. 8 © Huber Images/Zuma Press; p. 12 James A. Sugar/National Geographic/Getty Images; pp. 15, 36 Library of Congress Prints and Photographs Division; p. 18 Henry Guttmann/Hulton Archive/Getty Images; pp. 21, 34 © AP Images; p. 22 Stock Montage/Getty Images; p. 24 © Wyoming State Archives; p. 26 © www.istockphoto.com/Jim W. Parkin; p. 27 Robert Nickelsberg/ Liaison/Getty Images; p. 28 © Jim West/Zuma Press; p. 30 Hulton Archive/Getty Images; p. 31 Pascal Le Segretain/Getty Images; p. 39 (left) Courtesy of Robesus, Inc.; p. 40 (left) © www.istockphoto.com/Stephen Muskie; p. 40 (right) © www.istockphoto. com/Angela Cable.

Designer: Les Kanturek; Photo Researcher: Amy Feinberg